101 WAYS
TO SUPERVISE
LIKE A HUMAN BEING

by

Martin M. Broadwell
President,
Center for Management Services, Inc.

and

Carol Broadwell Dietrich
President,
Training Systems International, Inc.

authorHOUSE™

1663 LIBERTY DRIVE, SUITE 200
BLOOMINGTON, INDIANA 47403
(800) 839-8640
WWW.AUTHORHOUSE.COM

First published by AuthorHouse 07/22/05

ISBN: 1-4208-3625-0 (sc)

Library of Congress Control Number: 2005901710

Printed in the United States of America
Bloomington, Indiana

This book is printed on acid-free paper.

Prologue:

This book is the result of over forty years of both supervising and training supervisors all over the world. Hopefully, you won't have to read the whole book, since it's designed for you to go to it as a handbook of solutions for specific problems. Some of you may want to read it like a regular book. That'll work, too! Fortunately, the sections are small so you can read a few at a time, or just those where you feel you might get some help. Here's our wish for you: Supervision is a skill and can be learned. Not only that, even when you get good, you can still be better. For the sake of those people under you, We plead with you to work hard at being better at it. It's too bad, but most of what you will learn will come from your mistakes. Guess who gets to be the practice field while you are learning? Go easy on them, for their sake, as you get better. . .

Dedication:

To Norm Stanton, long time friend, merciless editor now retired, genius at his work, and the one who suggested this book. Any author should be so lucky as to have Norm doing your book! Guaranteed success! You can trust his choice of restaurants but watch out for his golf game!

To Margie Garrett, who not only makes you look good with her editing, but can also make it still sound your work! An excellent writer in her own fields, she knows how to lop off those dangling participles and corner those gerunds! Oh, and name any song: She can play it beautifully on the piano by ear, pop or classical.

To Denny Grumpler, a great friend to us both, dedicated to good training—himself or other—master of encouragement, and a fantastic family man. He's kept us straight in doing pre-leadership training for a couple of decades, and has trusted us with most of his future leaders. They don't come any better than Denny!

Table of Contents

Foreword

The layout of this book is simple. There are many things we can do to be better at supervision, even if we're already pretty good at it. The book is divided into six major sections:

1. Respect Our People
2. Praise Our People
3. Make our Corrections Constructive
4. Let Our Discipline Have Positive Results
5. Make our Delegation a Learning Experience
6. Manage Our Time To Our Advantage

Each of these sections contains some numbered specifications ("Tips") for improving our supervision. Following each of these are some sentences that expand on the idea and giving rationale.

One problem with learning to supervise better is that we're like the farmer being told how to farm better who replies: "Shucks, I ain't farming near as well as I know how, now!" There's not much in this book that's new. There's not much you haven't heard before. There's not much you haven't practiced in the past. So why the book? Simple enough: in the rush of everyday business, we forget some simple things and take short cuts, not only with things we do but also with the people we supervise. This book will remind us, in a simple way, of things we know will work, that we've seen work, yet tend to forget.

This is not a complicated book. It isn't a college text. It doesn't use any fancy words or phrases or gimmicks or "systems." The point of that is that supervisors need simple answers to simple problems. It's a fact that most frontline supervisors don't have any huge problems. They have lots of small problems that seem to make friends with other small problems; and when they get together, they can look pretty big! The truth is sometimes the problems seem so insignificant that they are overlooked or avoided. For example, if someone comes back from break a few minutes late a couple of times a week, what's the big deal? We ignore it and hope—like a stray dog that's ignored—it will go away. Sadly, unlike the stray dog, it won't go away, and it grows into a bigger animal as other employees begin to follow suit. Most supervisors have what look like big problems because they didn't deal with them when they were little. The object of this book is to suggest ways of preventing the little problems from growing, and hopefully to stop them from occurring in the first place.

101 Ways To Supervise Like A Human Being

Part One:
"Respect Our People"

1. *Treat our people like human beings, not cattle or numbers.*

Everybody brings a mind and a body to work. We want their minds to do the work. We want them thinking; and if it's a physical job, we want their minds telling their bodies what and how to do the job. If their mind is engaged in the activity, then it can tell them a better way or a safer way or a quicker way. Remember, people are the only resource we have that should get better with use! We have an obligation to not only use but to improve their minds so that this can happen. Sometimes we tend to think of them as simply "warm bodies," or so many cattle, instead of human beings with individual minds.

2. *Treat our people like we'd like to be treated.*

Too many of us have had bad bosses and then became a supervisor and begin to act just like our former boss. We didn't like that kind of supervising, so why should our people like it when we supervise the same way? If we didn't like being screamed at, are we so much better at screaming that our people like it? Our problem is that if a bad boss is our only role model we have had, and we don't have any other example of good supervision to go to for getting the work done in a crisis, we'll act the same way. But remember, we didn't like it, and it probably did affect our productivity.

3. *Treat our people like gold mines*

Dig for their abilities, their thinking power. Often the jobs we give people are so routine, so unchallenging, that our workers can do them and leave their minds at the door. Gold is seldom out on top of the ground in obvious view. It has to be discovered, dug up, even refined to become fine jewelry. People, like gold, are more effective when their true value is recognized, brought to the surface and treated correctly. They keep getting better all the time. Often people, like gold, have to be cleaned up and polished. So do our people. They don't always come in perfect condition. Like most things that are worthwhile, it often takes work to bring out the best. What's great about working with people, the potential never seems to run out.

4. *Treat people as valuable resources*

What other resource do we have that becomes more valuable the more we use it? We use up all the other resources, like wood, metal, money, paper, and even machines. People's performances, treated correctly, can continue to improve as long as we allow them to maximize their potential. They won't necessarily get better by themselves; they have to be guided, trained, and kept informed of the quality of their present work performance. Remember, if our people aren't continuing to improve, it reflects on us because we're accountable for all of our resources, including the human resource. We might ask ourselves, "How long would the organization accept it we were squandering away raw materials or money?" The answer is obvious and we watch the resources very carefully to get the most from all or any of it. The same should be true with the people resource we have working for us.

5. *Treat a person as someone who can continue to learn.*

Remember when we first started to work? We've learned a lot since then! When people quit learning, they start to be poorer workers. They lose their motivation and lose interest in not only their own job, but also the one they have the potential to attain. That means continuous training.

Give them the satisfaction of doing some things well, but always keep a challenge in the wings—something they can learn. Some have said that a day shouldn't go by that we don't learn something we didn't know when we showed up for work. The same should be true for the people reporting to us; they should be thought of as "learning machines," always on the lookout for something new. Of course, it's our job to see that it works this way!

6. *Treat our people like they have families, problems, likes and dislikes.*

They have burned toast, too! They have monthly bills, problem children and arguments with their spouse—just like we do. They aren't cattle, inhuman beings. They're just people trying to make a living and feed their families - and usually trying to get ahead. They have kids to send to college, dreams of retirement, and hopes of meaningful accomplishments. We can either stand in the way or help them meet those goals. When it finally dawns on us that the people working for us—all of them—are not that much different from us, things will get better in the relationship. Oddly enough, even if we came up through the ranks, working side-by-side with the folks now reporting to us, we have a hard time relating to them as real people just like us. Somehow we manage to get ourselves above them, rather than realize that but for a few different events, our job could be theirs, not ours. . .

7. *Treat our people as though they want to succeed.*

Make it a self-fulfilling prophecy. People tend to become what we expect of them. If we expect poor performance, we will probably get poor performance. Expect growth and contribution and that's what we'll get. Constantly review their performance and find where they do, or could, excel. Build on their strengths. Make it happen by challenge, and by praise and recognition when they do achieve some success.

Try this little experiment: pick five of your people and write down where you think they will be two years from now. Now, being honest with yourself, see if you're treating these people differently because of that view (good or bad). Are you giving the challenging assignments only to those you think have greater potential? And conversely, the mundane or non-challenging jobs to those you feel have less potential? If so, then realize that you are helping to contribute to making the "self-fulfilling prophecy" come true. We can heavily influence it either way!

8. *Give our people an opportunity to know what else there is for them.*

Talk about the future, not the past. Talk about the present in relationship to the future. "Here's where you could be in the future," is a heart-warming statement. Let them know there is something out there they can have, if they want to work for it. Any performance evaluation should always look ahead to achieved goals being put to work on future projects. The deficiencies should be seen as opportunities to grow, building on the strengths already demonstrated. If they are doing well on something, use that to improve a weakness. For example, if someone has good communication skills, yet runs disorganized safety meetings, train them in organization skills for those meetings, utilizing their communication skills.

9. *Give our people opportunities to succeed.*

Gradually expand their jobs into areas where we know they can be successful, with a little help. Be sure that we reward them with praise when they accomplish an additional task. Remember, the more they do of the doing, the more we can do of the planning they're doing. Get them planning, too. Mutually agree on their doing a task for which they'll have to learn a new procedure or skill, find new sources of information, or find additional people to coordinate with. Make it as exciting, as possible and be sure to reward good results along the way.

10. *Give our people a safe area in which to fail.*

Let them know it's all right to fail if it's a new assignment and they do their best. Make it a learning experience, not a punishing one. "Okay, let's see what we've learned from this," is the way we need to approach either a failure or a success. Be sure they discover not only why they failed, but also what they can learn from the experience. They need to recognize the obstacles that could cause them to fail the next time. Of course, the object here isn't to fail; it's to allow the employee to learn from trying something new. If they succeed, so much the better! If they go into the new effort with a fear of failure, their motivation will be very low. On the other hand, if they go into the assignment knowing that the goal is to learn a new skill they will be using on the job, but also knowing they may fail the first time or two, they will be more attentive to succeeding than failing.

11. *Teach our people to swim BEFORE we throw them in over their heads.*

Training is better than trial and error. They may learn to dog-paddle when we throw them in over their heads, but that's also a pretty good way to drown them. Time is too short and the job too important to let someone fail for the sake of learning. Training them to do it right the first time is much sounder. Too many times we find ourselves too busy to take the time to train properly. We hand them a manual or sit them with someone else, and expect learning to take place. No matter how good the manuals may be, there's no way the manual can check to see if things were being done correctly. The same is true of sitting them with someone else. Just because someone knows the job, doesn't mean they are good at training a person to do the job. We need to either do the training or supervise the training so we'll know what is being trained. By the way, the training should be good training. We need to remember that training is a skill in itself and, like any other skill, can be done well or poorly. Training is a learned skill!

12. *We need to get to know our people.*

No two people are exactly alike, hence they will not always react the same way. Some like close supervision; others like to go it alone as much as possible. Some get their feelings hurt and sulk for a few days at the slightest criticism; others may laugh it off and try harder the next time. People who are poorly motivated need us to be their motivation. Sometimes praise will do it; at other times correction in the form of constructive feedback is needed. Sometimes letting them make their own decisions about doing the job will help, but sometimes it will just frighten them. The point is that the better we get to know the person behind the face, the better chance we'll have of supervising them correctly. So called "personality conflicts" most often occur when we just don't take the time to get to know the other person. It's amazing how much better we get along with a person when we know where their hang-ups are, and what their psychic needs are.

13. *Lead our people as a friend, not as an enemy*

We don't have to like all the people who work for us, but if we don't, it doesn't make them our enemy. (They may not like us, either!) If they're doing what they're supposed to do, the way it's supposed to be done, and aren't bothering other employees, that's what we're paying them to do. They aren't paid to like us or to become likeable themselves. We can get into trouble when we start creating personal relationships with employees. We are first a member of management, second we are their supervisor, third, we may be their friend. Getting to know someone doesn't mean we have to know their personal life, their family situations, how much money they owe, and what's hidden deep inside their closets. What we do have to know is how to best communicate to the person, what kind of things are motivating and what things turn them off. It may not always work, but it's worth the try.

14. *Find good things about everyone.*

There is a good reason why they got the job and some good reasons why they're still on the job. We should build on the good qualities that got them there and are keeping them there. We need to remember that 99% of what the people are doing is correct or they shouldn't be there at all. Often our problem is that the good is less obvious than the bad, so we see the bad first. If we keep looking, we'll be surprised at how much good there is. (If we can't find the good, then maybe we're the one who is at fault, because we've kept them around so long!) The truth is, we see the bad more easily than the good. We have to look harder for the good because the bad jumps out at us while the good is just the routine doing of the job. Still, we have to find the good if we're going to use it to build a better employee.

15. *Give our people some leeway to be out of sorts occasionally.*

We have expectations and standards, but we all get cross sometimes. Just don't let it become a habit for us or them. If the person is most often easy to get along with, cut some slack when he or she is occasionally cross. They've earned the right to be human and have a bad moment or a bad day. The irony is that the employees have more right to be cross than we do. As the supervisor, we can't afford to be cross because it affects everyone, not just one person. Of course, we're talking about the occasional cross person or out-of-sorts person. Consistent malcontents need to be dealt with early and well. Remember, the organization has some standards of behavior, usually written, which everyone should meet; however, we, as the supervisor, can add our own, as long as they don't conflict with the organization's. That includes setting some standards of how people talk to each other and to us.

16. *Be honest with our people.*

Use tact, but tell the truth, even if it is painful for them and us. Nothing beats a reputation of being fair and honest. It's nice to deserve that reputation, but nicer still to have it and still be able to correct mistakes without embarrassment. If we don't have an answer, we should make a serious effort to find it, rather than fake an answer that we have to come back and change later. Obviously there are times when we can't reveal everything we know, because of policy or procedures changes. But we should be careful not to let our knowledge be a substitute for power. Withholding information to gain power over the group isn't very smart and certainly wears down morale. The more we share and be open with our employees, the more they'll understand when we can't reveal all we know.

17. *Don't forget to be the boss.*

Whatever else we are, we're still the boss. We may continue to eat with them, go hunting with them, and carpool with them, but still they know they're eating and hunting and riding with the boss. And that's the way it should be. We're paid to be their supervisor, their leader, their boss. Because of that, we must not act the part—we have to be the part. They know, as well as we know that we have to answer for their performance, and can be considered good or bad based on just that: "How well did my people do?" We have to supervise and lead and be their boss. Just being a likeable, "good ole boy" or "good ole girl" won't get that message across. This doesn't mean we have to lord it over them; nor does it mean we can't be pleasant and likeable.

18. *Don't use being the "boss" as a club*

Anyone who does the job right because "we say so," won't do it right when we aren't there "to say so!" We need to build confidence in the job, in the person doing the job and in ourselves. Theodore Roosevelt is credited with saying that the different between a "boss and a leader is that the boss drives, the leader leads." It doesn't take much skill to drive people or to get them to do something because we have the power to make them do it, but it takes a lot of skill to get them to do the job because they want to—and want to do it right. Of course some people do things right because they respect the boss and want to please him or her. There's nothing wrong with this, but the best world is the one where they want to do the job because it's their job and they feel it's their job.

19. *Use our heart sometimes instead of our head.*

We don't have to be gushy to be compassionate. Our understanding and caring is essential to our people. We don't have to let it rule our judgment, or keep us from dealing with poor performers, but even these dealings can be done in a caring way. Certainly it can be overdone, but usually we are so far from overdoing it, the dangers are small. We need to remember that these are people, human beings with feelings and concerns and problems—just like us! There's always the chance that what appears to us to be a small problem may be a very large one to them. If we handle the situation incorrectly, it will become a large problem for them. If we scream to get it done more quickly or because of errors, we'll make it big because we didn't understand their deeper feeling about what they were trying to do.

20. *For better understanding, try to think and feel like they do.*

By simply asking ourselves, "How would I feel if I were being treated like this?" we can build understanding. If we use our memory a little we can probably think of a time when we were in a situation similar to theirs, and either got understanding or didn't. We can decide quickly which is best! Sympathy is much better when it has empathy for a companion. It's amazing how soon we forget what it's like in their place. The old adage about walking in someone else's shoes to understand them is a good one, but harder to do than it seems. We may not have worked in the exact same job; we may not have worked for someone like us; we may not have worked with the same kind of people or the same kind of company. Any one of these will make it hard for us to walk in their shoes. Still, we have had supervision and still do. We can ask ourselves, how would I like my boss to treat me—right now—if I had the same problems facing me. We are quick to tell someone, "If I were you, I'd do so and so." What we really mean is, "If you were me, you'd do so and so." I probably don't know what I'd do if I were them, because I don't think like they do.

How To Supervise Like A Human Being

Part 2:
"Praise Your People"

21. *Tell them when they do a good job.*

We all like to be told when we do well, even if we already know it.

While some may need more psychic rewards than others, few people are hurt by it, even if they don't need it. Interestingly, praise is one of the most effective motivators, from an impact standpoint; but it's duration isn't very long. That works in our favor as a supervisor, because it means we can use it again, get the same impact, even shortly after the last time. And we can continue to use it. The key, of course, is to make certain that we're praising something that they've actually done well. It's not just a matter of going down the line to each person and saying, "Good job, good job, good job." We praise them for something they are doing that we like, something that meets standard, something that we'd like for them to continue to do as they are doing it now.

22. *Make doing well a pleasant experience.*

We all tend to repeat those behaviors that are pleasant or satisfying to us. Certainly, our people are paid for working —even doing a good job—but the ten seconds to say, "Good job" isn't going to cost us much time, money or effort. People rarely get tired of being told they're doing well. There are few documented cases where people have left a job because the boss is always telling them they're doing a good job. There are millions of documented cases where people left their jobs because they weren't appreciated or the boss never praised them. But let's suppose for a moment we do tell them too often—however times too often would be—we're still ahead of the game. Think of the impact it will have on them when we have to correct them! It will certainly get their attention quickly enough, and make our job easier, since they know we are honest with them, good or bad.

23. *We have to look for the good things people do.*

We see the bad things people do all the time, but we have to look for the good. Whatever the reason for that is, it tells us that seeing the things done wrong or poorly is easier than finding things done right. We need to walk around occasionally just looking for the good things, without mentioning the bad. It may surprise us to see how much is being done at or above standard. We don't even have to mention the bad at this time; there'll be plenty of time for that later, if it's necessary. Some feel that they shouldn't give too much praise because the employees will start to slack off. There's isn't much evidence to support this, and it's usually a cop out to explain why we don't use more praise.

Try this: List a couple of employees who work for you, no matter how well or poorly they are doing. Under each name, write down at lest five things they have done well or correctly in the last two days. Now put a check mark by the ones we've told them how well they're doing. Chances are there'll be more we haven't mentioned than those we have. This tells us there's always something out there we can praise them for.

24. *Find more good things than bad our people are doing.*

Criticism wears people down; praise builds them up. It takes a lot of praise to overcome just one criticism, and we remember the criticism much longer than the praise. If criticism is deserved and needed, we have to do it; but there are ways of making even criticism positive. We should be using "Constructive Feedback." It isn't just a fancy way of criticizing someone; the idea of "constructive" says the end result is going to be a behavior change for the good, so it is positive. We tend to praise our good employees more than the bad ones, even for the same job done well. For whatever reason, this isn't fair and is simply giving more motivation to the good employee than the poor one. It should be obvious that if praise works, it works on the poor performer, who probably hasn't had nearly as much as the above average employee—throughout life, not just in this job.

25. *We should praise specifically, not generally.*

Tell our people exactly what they're doing well, not just, "You're doing a good job." Since people tend to repeat the things that are satisfying—and praise is satisfying—we want the good things they are doing to be repeated. This means we need to make certain they know what they're doing that we like. "That was a good suggestion about how to handle overtime on this special project" welcomes more suggestions. A nebulous, "Good job," without specifics feels good, but it may leave them wondering just what it was we liked. That makes it hard to repeat! There should never be any doubt about what they're doing that we like, what it is that has generated praise on our part. Remember, we can praise them for doing the job correctly with consistency, even if they aren't exceeding standards. "You know, Joanna, it's great that I can always know you'll finish on time and the work will be done just right. Thanks a lot for that!" Joanna may not be a real ball of fire. She may not be the one who comes up with the best suggestions. But she's on time with her work every time and I don't have to check on her. That makes Joanna a very valuable employee. She needs to know that I know that, and that I like it!

26. *We should praise only for the right things done well*

Unnecessary things, though they are done well, really aren't worth doing at all, and certainly not worth doing well. (Better read that again!) Some people find things they like to do and can do well, and spend a lot of time on them. Unfortunately, the things they are doing so well, isn't a part of their job description and isn't something they're supposed to be doing at all. To make it worse, they may be letting their real assignment go. While we appreciate them doing a good job and being consistent at it, we have a right to expect them to be doing their assigned work during working hours. When we praise the unnecessary accomplishment, we'll just get more of the unneeded work. Our job is to make certain the employee is doing what is needed and what is identified as his or her job; then when it's done well, praise it!

27. *Spread the praise around*

The majority of the people are doing the majority of things well, the majority of the time—or they wouldn't be there—so there's plenty of deserved praise to go around. There's no need for us to have to spend a lot of time trying to find out things people are doing well. By the same token, there's no reason for us to only praise a few, hand picked people to give praise to. This means that we can't just praise the people we like or those we want to see get ahead. Spreading the praise around and even praising the whole group as one entity helps to build a team. Fairness means we praise good work, no matter who does it, with no sarcasm or kidding. Remember, praise and correction are not things to joke about. It is just as serious when people do well as when they foul up. We can keep it that way by not kidding, being sarcastic, or using ridicule. "Well, Joe, I see you finally got it right for a change. Thanks a lot," isn't exactly a proper form of praise! Joe probably isn't going to be really fired up to do it right the next time.

28. *Praise for actual performance.*

"Promiscuous" praise usually gets wasted, so we praise for real things. Simply put, praise good work that we'd like to see repeated. Encourage people when they are doing what they were hired to do and what we want them to continue doing. When we see them working or think about their job as we ride to work in the morning, say to ourselves, "What are they doing right? What are they doing well? What are they doing that really needs to be done well?" (We tend to say, "What are they doing wrong? What are they doing that I need to get on them for? What are they not doing that they should be doing?") It's a frame of mind that we have to work on getting into. It's so natural to see bad things, but if we look for actual things being done properly, the job gets easier. When we see people doing something well— something that is their assigned task—we simply say, "You're doing that really well. Thanks!"

29. *Praise in Public*

Without being too blaring, we can appeal to ego by letting others know an employee has done well. We don't have to make such a big show of it that it becomes embarrassing to the employee. However, we ought to be willing to say the same thing to others who perform just as well. Some employees act as though they don't want to be praised in public, but many times that is just a front. The simpler we keep it, the better it is and the more impact it has. Walking by an employee, with others around, and say, "Doug, thanks for helping out last night on that project. We made it on time!" Doug knows how we feel; the other employees know that one of their buddies did something well, and nobody should be embarrassed. Keep doing it till they protest seriously. They may not know how to react because they aren't used to being praised at all, much less in public! That's our fault, not theirs, because we may not have done it often enough, with enough of our people.

30. *Praise in private.*

Whether in public or in private, praise is between the boss and employee. Sometimes a "nice work" pat on the back or a "good job" handshake is more significant in private. It's a special moment that brings it closer to the employee with almost no words. It has to be sincere, and it has to be for a special assignment or a difficult task that the employee has handled in a superior manner. If the employee wants others to know, he or she can tell them. There's no secret about it, nor are we trying to hide it. It's just that sometimes there is something special about the relationship between the boss and employee where they've worked hard as a team, gotten a job done right and on time, and a good handshake means more than a lot of fanfare and hoopla in front of everybody else. There are times when public praise means a lot, of course, but these special moments also give good feelings and mean a lot to the employee.

31. *Document praise.*

We have to remember that good things need to be on record, too, maybe even more than bad things. So often we find that the personnel files are full of warnings, and reprimands, or nothing. We shouldn't record just what people have done badly. We need to record the good things for performance appraisal time. Remember that all of our employees are doing more good things than bad ones. We don't have to load them down with comments every time they do something good, but if it's good enough to commend them for, at least occasionally there should be something worthy of documenting. It doesn't make a lot of sense to record when a person comes in ten mintes late, yet make no mention of them coming in on time everyday for a year! This ought to be an ongoing thing, making note of achievements of our people. We certainly don't have to save the recording of good things till performance evaluation time, and we surely want the employee to know that the good things are going on record as well as any less-than-standard efforts.

32. *Give written praise for "showing around."*

A simple "Thanks, Good Work" note on top of a good report, or a "stick 'em" note on the desk in the morning can be put on the refrigerator at home for family viewing, on the cubicle wall, or even left on the desk where others can "accidentally" see it. This is a good way to read our employees as to their psychic needs. If they just throw it in the waste basket or stick it in the drawer, it probably means they are reasonably secure in their job and outlook. They're probably not short on psychic rewards. It they leave if for others to see, it may mean they enjoy others knowing they have been praised. This doesn't mean that we don't praise them or quit leaving notes for them. We aren't doing it to psychoanalyze them; we're doing it because their work deserves praise. We do it because it's the right thing to do.

33. *Send a note "upstairs" about good performance.*

Higher management likes to know about good things every once in a while, and employees like for them to know it, too! We can hope that higher management will also make a marginal note as evidence it's been to the top! At least two positive things come from this. First, top management is getting a view of our people in a favorable light; Second, top management know that there is a potential worker that may be able to take our place if an opening becomes available. With top management signing off with a note of recognition—often with our encouragement—it leaves a large amount of motivation in the wake! We get another chance to give recognition if the boss puts a note on ours. We pass it back to the employee saying, "Note the boss' remark."

34. *Include praise in general correspondence*

If the performance is a significant contribution, mention it in regular reports or memos. A quote like, "By the way, I'd like to mention that Susan did an outstanding job on the last quarterly report. Accounting was high in their praise. Thanks Susan!" really goes a long way in letting people know they are appreciated. A couple of extra sentences is a small price to pay for the encouragement it brings. Again, we have to be willing to do this for anyone who makes a contribution that's meaningful to everyone, not just the high achiever. It not only lets the others on the team what a team member has done well, but lets them know that the organization recognizes good work. They, too, can get that kind of recognition!

35. *Spread the word through others.*

"Hey, Bob, when you see Al tell him the Bryson job turned out great!" The situation is that Al did a super job on the Bryson project and we haven't had an opportunity to talk to him yet. We see Bob in the corridor and tell him to tell Al what we said. If we do it this way, it lets others know of the good performance of a co-worker. Usually we reserve praise and constructive feedback for us to say ourselves, but it's a good idea every once in a while to let others pass the word to a fellow employee. We'll still want to talk to Al about his work, rather than him getting only second hand information. It's a subtle way to let others know without making a federal case out of the situation. Of course, this doesn't eliminate our obligation to talk directly to the good performer; otherwise it just becomes "hearsay," not our direct communication.

36. *Use the telephone or e-mail for praise.*

Any way we can get to employees to tell them they've done a good job is a good way to go. The telephone is quick, and it's much more personal than electronic mail, but e-mail works, too. A simple, "Chuck, just to thank you for the good performance in the staff meeting this morning. You were right on target with those figures," will make somebody's day. Don't run it in the ground, but remember we rarely get complaints about using too much praise. We're talking about only ten to fifteen seconds of our time for a much longer lasting motivational tool. Besides, good work deserves as much of our time as we can spare! Electronic mail gets overused, but it does make it possible for the raised individual to save the message and/or send it along to others.

37. *Praise for things other than performance, too.*

"Thanks for volunteering to stay over late last night. It sure did relieve some pressure from all of us." Anything that's above and beyond the call of duty is worthy of praise—since we hope it will be repeated. This also includes superior attitudes. "Hey, Walt, that was neat the way you picked up the slack yesterday when Brad had to go home sick. Thanks!" It can be short, public or private, but always right to the point. Simple willingness to cooperate in something that isn't normally the person's job, deserves some recognition. While we tend to spend most of our time with poor performers, and only occasionally praise outstanding performers, it's the "average-always-there-always-meeting-the-standards" employees who make the work go, day in and day out. These people need our praise!

38. *Praise consistency as well as above average performance.*

People who are never late, always smile, or never have dirty work stations are worthy of praise, though it's listed as "standard" behavior. Since we are totally dependent on the vast majority of our people who are average, do their jobs right the first time, are there on time, but may not exceed the standards too often, we need to recognize them for being just that: being dependable. Praising this behavior gives us a chance to take care of some routine-but-important aspects of the workforce, like being on time, meeting deadlines consistently, or coming up with simple, practical ideas. It goes like this: "Janna, I really appreciate your approach to any task I assign you. You always say, 'Great, let's get started!' That sure makes my job easier!" Obviously, it's not enough just to smile and act willing. There has to be work that's up to standard that we're praising, not just the smile!

41

39. *Praise corrected performance immediately.*

The sole purpose of constructive feedback is to correct—or change behavior for good—so when employees respond and make that change, we need to reward them with praise as soon as it happens. That will encourage it's happening again, and it leaves the employee feeling better for having made the change. The constructive feedback wasn't punishment—it was our effort to get a change in behavior from unsatisfactory to satisfactory. The employees will know that we noticed and appreciated the change to good behavior just as quickly as we noticed the poor performance that led to the corrective comments. However, we shouldn't dwell on the past history when praising the change in behavior. "Thanks, Bill, that's a lot better than the poor way you've been doing it," loses something as far as praise is concerned! Talk about what's being done correctly. "Thanks, Bill. Good job!" says it all. Bill knows that he was at fault and he knows that we know. Now it's time for him to know that we like what he's doing, so lets get on with the job.

40. *Keep the praise simple.*

Praise is important, but it counts only if the employee knows that we know he or she has done a good job. Praise doesn't have to be elaborate; it doesn't mean getting up on the table and shouting about it. A simple, "Thank you!" may be all that's needed. Naturally, if it's a big deal we're praising, the praise should be a big deal, too. Probably the worst mistake we can make it to start to increase the size of the reward each time. We start of with a small star on the good letter that's been written. Then a bigger star, then an even bigger star, and pretty soon the whole letter is one big star. Or we reward a performance with a cup of coffee on the house, then break, then lunch, and pretty soon we're taking the whole department out to dinner. To avoid this, we may even go in reverse sometimes. Maybe we take them on break, but the next time it's a hearty handshake. Avoid making it an "entitlement," something they expect, and start looking for yet a bigger reward.

41. *Build a team with group praise.*

While it's important that each person get praised for his or her individual work, we need to remember that much of what our people do has to be a coordinated effort. This means that often times one person's contribution affects all the others. It's important that there be some good natured competition between individuals, but it's also very important that we have some competition between departments or other groups. Letting the groups as a whole know when they've done well as a team, helps build that team and strengthens it's cohesion. Outperforming the day shift may not deserve a family outing, but it may deserve bringing in donuts for everyone and letting them know we're proud of them.

101 Ways To Supervise Like A Human Being

Part Three:
Constructive Feedback

42. *Use "Constructive Feedback" instead of criticism."*

Good, dependable employees still may mess up occasionally, not necessarily on purpose, and not necessarily in a big way. But if we see a pattern developing, like taking too long on breaks two or three times a week, then we need to correct that behavior. "Criticism" calls attention to the poor performance, but it isn't a positive solution. "Constructive" aims at improving the behavior; "Feedback" is simply letting the person know not only the observed behavior but also a standard that's expected. The object of Constructive Feedback is to give the employee a look at their performance measured against the standard of performance expected of them. It gives a goal and an expectation of meeting that goal. Criticism, on the other hand, just focuses on the poor performance, without a plan for improvement.

43. *Correct Behavior, not attitudes*

One major fault of performance evaluation, both formal and informal, is that it often deals with attitudes. The classic statement in appraisals is, "Well, Charlie, your work is fine, but you've got a lousy attitude!" The fact is that attitudes can't be measured without talking about behavior. No one is hired under a contract that specifies that they must have a "good attitude" all the time. When we try to define someone's attitude by saying someone is late all the time, grumbles a lot, talks bad about the company, or always has a sullen look., we are really talking about behavior, not attitudes. As a supervisor, we can require our people to be on time and insist that they not spend their time complaining about assignments we give them, or not use others' time talking about the company, etc. If we're in customer relations, we may have a requirement that the employee present a smile to the customers and not a frown. That's not dealing with attitude; it's dealing with required performance.

44. *We should discipline people, not punish them.*

Many of us make the mistake of thinking of discipline as a form of punishment, just as we do at times with our children. Punishment is making someone pay for transgressing a rule or a policy. It's done by losing privileges or making up in some other way for the wrong deed they have done. That's shouldn't be true in the work world. The purpose of discipline is to change the behavior of the employee so that he or she is performing to the stated and set standard. Ideally, if we don't yet have a standard and the employee is attempting to do the job, we let that employee have considerable input into setting the standard. The truth is, many of us still think in terms of punishment rather than discipline. We're unhappy that the employee has messed up so we feel a need to punish him or her. What our concern should be is changing the employee's performance to meet job standards.

45. *We should judge behavior in terms of a stated standard.*

Despite of our best efforts, we sometimes wait to set a standard till we see something being done which we don't like. Either we just never thought about setting a standard on a job that's been around for a long time, or we've never seen the need before. We may even say something like, "Well, everybody knows how that's supposed to be done." That may be all right, providing we aren't judging the employee's performance at the same time. That's about as ridiculous as having the traffic cop say, "We've just decided to lower the speed limit along here and will be putting the signs up tomorrow. Since you were exceeding that new limit you've violated the law!" The process is simple:

1)Set the standard,

2)Inform the workers,

3)Then evaluate the employee against that standard!

Of course, that assumes the employee understands and has been trained to meet that standard.

46. *We begin correction by stating the observed, incorrect behavior.*

The first step in changing the behavior of an employee who is seen doing something incorrectly (violating the standard) is to state the observed behavior. There should be no mysteries about why we're talking to the employee at this time about this action. After describing what we saw, it is then time to listen to the employee's reaction. We aren't looking for justification or excuses—just a statement letting the employee know that there was a problem with his or her behavior, then getting the employee's view of the problem. "Tom, I noticed you were about ten minutes late the last two mornings. Is there a problem?" We don't argue the point— we just listen. Remember, this is a satisfactory employee who has messed up for the first time.

47. *We state the standard for our correction, and the reason for the standard.*

"Tom, I noticed you were about ten minutes late the last two mornings. Is there a problem?" This is what we said when we decided to do some constructive feedback. We're in the process of stating the standard and giving the reason for that standard. No matter what Tom says in this case, we listen, then state the standard: "Well, Tom, the standard is that everyone needs to be here by 8:00 o'clock." Then we state the reason for the standard: "That way, no one has to wait for anyone else when there is some coordination to be done." We need to understand that the key here is to be sure the employee knows the standard. If not then it's time for explanation and/or training. The truth is we can't really hold an employee accountable for a standard he or she doesn't know, doesn't understand, and hasn't been trained to do. However, when we have explained the standard and made certain the employee understands it and knows how to do it, we must then hold the employee accountable for doing it.

48. *We use their strengths to improve deficiencies.*

The hard part of correcting employees includes finding a way to help them improve. It is important not to use the correction against them, but as a means of improving. "Sue, you're a very good writer. Your choice of words and organization is excellent. If you can apply that skill and knowledge to conducting meetings, you'll find a great match. This will really put you on top of the meeting business!" Our tendency is to separate the two with "but" which loses the value of both efforts. "Sue, you are a very good writer, Your choice of words and organization is excellent, but you don't seem to use that skill when you're conducting meetings." The compliment gets lost in the criticism.

49. *Point out to good performers that this behavior isn't like them.*

Remember, we're talking about a good employee who has messed up enough that we need to deal with it, not with a poor performer or one whom we must constantly correct. This is an unusual situation and, in a way, not a big deal. We need to pass this information on to the employee. "Tom, when we're talking about your tardiness, we aren't talking about formal discipline. I mention it because it just isn't like you to be late." The two points are; "It's no big deal," and "It isn't like you." Sure, being late is a big deal, if it's a habit. It's not a big deal when it's happened only a couple of times in the last two or three weeks. If it's something we've had to talk to Tom about several times before, it is a big deal and it may lead to formal discipline.

50. *We should remember that most people don't mess up on purpose.*

Start with the assumption that people get careless or forget, or that they are untrained, distracted, or uncertain of what to do—and mess up. Only a very few do it on purpose. It's important to remember that we're talking about "Constructive Feedback" which is a means of doing day-to-day supervision. It's an effort to get a good employee back on the right track from a minor infraction. There's no "attitude" problem here. There's no intentional violation of a cardinal rule. The employee has just messed up a little—enough to require it to be mentioned. The truth is, we all mess up sometimes. We don't do it on purpose and we're usually sorry we did it, but it happens. For that reason we need to make the constructive feedback as brief and concise as possible and go on with the work of the day.

51. *We should be certain not to feed stray dogs.*

One of the best ways to get a pet that will stay around is to feed a stray dog. After a few feedings, it becomes a permanent fixture, whether or not we want it to. The point? When we let employees—even good employees—continue with a bad habit (not meeting standard or violating the standard) and don't take any action, we're feeding the stray dog. Not only will that behavior stay around, but others will also pick up on the lack of correction and assume it's all right to do the same thing. Pretty soon we have a whole pack of stray dogs! The problem here may be that the infraction seems minor and we just ignore it, hoping it'll go away. Ignoring it is the same as feeding a stray dog. It isn't likely to go away. The more we feed it, the harder it's going to be to get rid of it. We've allowed a habit to begin forming and habits are hard to break.

52. *Don't correct when angry.*

We should avoid emotional reactions to poor performance. No matter how much we abhor the action of the employee, most of us aren't good enough to deal properly with such a serious matter when we're angry. We may even say the right words, but our emotions will show through and give a bad impression. We just rarely think or say the right things when we are angry or upset. We may need to walk it off, count to a few thousand, wait till tomorrow. In most cases anything is better than an emotional confrontation. Dealing with serious problems when we're in an emotional state, most often causes either more problems or more serious problems than we had to start with. In the end, we find ourselves solving problems we caused while trying to solve the original one. It's sort of like treating the side effect of medicine we've taken for another ailment.

53. *Deal with consequences of nonstandard performance.*

Correction includes showing the employee the consequences of continued poor performance. It could even lead to Formal Discipline. "If this continues, Fred, we may have to go into formal discipline, which is much more serious." If it does continue, we have to deal with it in a more severe way, and it really can get into formal discipline—beyond just day-to-day supervision. That's neither where we want to go nor where the good employee wants to go. He or she needs to know the consequences and how to avoid them. The thing that happens all too often is that we ignore it, making the behavior appear as satisfactory. Then we have to over a problem that may have, by now, gotten much more serious than it should be. Small problems tend to get ignored—but nearly always make friends with other small ones—and appear as very large problems. We made them that way!

54. *Match standards with observed behavior.*

When we use the proper steps in constructive feedback, essentially we're saying, "This is what you're supposed to do; this is what I saw you doing this morning. They weren't the same." We may not be that blunt, but the employee must not have any doubt about either what the standard is or how his or her behavior differs from that standard. Again, this works only if the standards exist and are doable, measurable and observable. It also works only if the employees know the standard and have been trained to meet it—and we've actually seen them doing it correctly! It's one thing to tell them and assume they know, understand and can do it. (We know we're in trouble when we see them doing it wrong, and say, "Don't you remember I showed you exactly how to do this the other day!")

55. *Match performance with standards, not other employees.*

One major problem supervisors at all levels have is judging or measuring employees against other employees instead of by the standard. There's nothing fair about hiring an employee, stating the standard of expectation, training that person on the standard, and then evaluating the work by saying, "You know, Sheila, the others are really producing more than you're doing. They all exceed the standards except you." That amounts to us raising the standard! If the only way to be a satisfactory employee is to do more than standard, then that's the new standard. It's all right to have a competitive situation where employees try to outdo the others—as long as it's a healthy competition—but that's true only if everyone has been trained properly.

56. *"Constructive Feedback" is the day-to-day solution to incorrect behavior.*

Remember, these tips have been dealing with "Constructive Feedback." That's not discipline; it's keeping employees performing to standard, day-to-day. We're talking about good employees who have messed up some way. We're talking about dealing with small infractions which come from carelessness, oversight or just not paying attention to the job. We all recognize that this happens sometimes and we can either ignore it and let it become a bigger problem—with others picking up the habit—or we can deal with it and probably end the problem right there. Good supervisors use constructive feedback and positive reinforcement till the performance changes or gets beyond where these things work. In most cases it will improve. If not, we go on to a more severe form of behavior change effort—Formal Discipline.

57. *Praise is essential when poor behavior is changed.*

Okay, so we're doing pretty well in the day-to-day supervision. We look for things people are doing well and give positive recognition for it. They continue to do well because we've given them satisfaction for doing right. If someone messes up, we use constructive feedback to remind them of the standard. And that works, too! They change their behavior back to doing the job correctly. So we go on our way happy with our supervision? Wrong!! Of all the times for positive reinforcement, this is it. We must go back and reward this change in behavior as soon as possible. "Diane, I really appreciate the way your accuracy is hitting the mark consistently. You're really doing good work! Thanks for your effort." The employee must know that the proper change has been made, that the job is now being done satisfactorily, and that we as the supervisor know all of this.

58. *Any correction must deal with the future, not belabor the past.*

All correction should end on a positive note. "I'm sure we will see a change, now that you know the standards." This isn't the time to bring up past misdeeds. Avoid saying things like, "Now that I've explained the standards, I hope you'll do better than you've been doing." The best measure of our success at positive reinforcement is to be sure both of us feel good when it's over. That's what we mean when we call it "positive" reinforcement. The feedback is positive because we want this to be a kind of self-fulfilling prophecy. We state our expectation as an established fact, not a dream or some kind of hope-it-will-happen arrangement. This way it's more likely to happen than if we express concern that it may not turn out as we say it should.

101 Ways To Supervise Like A Human Being

Part Four:
Discipline

59. *Continued poor performance should lead to Formal Discipline.*

When employees consistently perform poorly, after discussion, training and explanations of standards, it's time to get into formal discipline. Generally, two things cause us to move on from Constructive Feedback or plain day-to-day supervision: 1) the frequency of the wrong behavior continues, even when there has been repeated effort to change the performance with constructive feedback and/or, 2) the other employees are somehow being affected. Either they are distracted or upset by the infractions, or they are having to fill in for lack of performance by the poor performer. That takes us to the Formal Discipline. We aren't officially in it till we tell the employee we are now there and explain the consequences of each step. Formal discipline is just that: There are steps and procedures including documentation. All of this goes on the employee's record and the Human Resources department is involved.

60. *Interference with other employees must be dealt with promptly*

"No man (or woman) is an island." Performing improperly around others will invariably cause problems. It may be distraction or frustration, or just general curiosity; but whatever it is, it's unfair to the other employees if we don't deal with the culprit quickly. That not only includes poor performance of the job itself, but also interference by talking, griping, mouthing off to others. The hazard is that when one person gets involved or distracted, soon another and then others are affected, and so on it goes. It's too big a risk to take. And speaking of risk, there's the safety issue. The distraction or loss of routine offers severe consequences if there are safety issues to be dealt with. Remember, we're talking about something that has happened before and is continuing to happen. It must be handled quickly and totally. It's important that the employee involved change behavior before the results are detrimental to both the job and the other people.

61. *Don't make up history for correction*

Document observations and discussions about the problem as they happen, not when it's time to begin discipline. Manufactured history is hard to defend. No matter how small the incidences of poor performance seem at the time, we ask ourselves, "If this continues, do I pursue discipline?" Even if we don't perceive that discipline will be required, we need to consider documenting the performance. Of course, that means we also record the good stuff. Fairness demands that we record the good things people do, and also that we use positive reinforcement or praise when it's deserved. Our documentation must also deal with actual events, not generalities filled with absolutes! "Mary, you are always late!". If she's ever been on time in her life, this is not a true statement! The more precise the observations are, the more reliable and helpful they'll be at discipline time. "Sometimes has errors in his accounting efforts," won't do the job.

62. *Never play "Gotcha" with discipline.*

Don't look for bad things in order to stick it to an employee. Keep looking for the good as well as the bad. If an employee is performing poorly, and the behavior is observable and violates standards, then we need to deal with it. However, if others are doing the same way, we must also deal with them. If we let others get away with the same behavior, we have to deal with all of those doing this, or none of them! Trying to "get" an employee always comes back to haunt us. It's unfair, dishonest and very, very unethical. Yet we still find ourselves doing it—often unawares. We either don't like the employee or there's a personality conflict of some sort, hence we fall into the trap of trying to figure out how to get something on the employee. The goal may be to get even, or to get rid of the employee. Either is unjustified. The simple rule is to deal with the facts—all the facts. This will include both the good and bad performances.

63. *Don't play favorites with discipline.*

We need to treat everyone with the same set of rules. We need to hold everyone to the same standards. Just because we don't like an individual, or want to get rid of the person, we don't have the right to deal unfairly with him or her in order to meet our needs. It may not be easy. Sometimes it may be impossible, but as far as discipline is concerned, we need to keep personalities out of our dealings. Discipline is serious business and often goes on the employee's record to their detriment. If they are really messing up and if we've got legitimate documentation, we aren't being unfair to deal with the person with formal discipline. Worse, yet, if it's a pretty good employee who has been one of our favorites, but is now consistently performing poorly and doesn't respond to constructive feedback, we still have to take the necessary action.

64. *Always leave a way out in discipline*

In order to get the person's attention, we need to make each step in formal discipline more and more severe. At first, it may be a simple verbal warning. The next step will be a written warning, which is more severe and is getting closer to even termination. However, if a change of behavior leads to a conclusion of the disciplinary steps, then we have to be prepared to go back to day-to-day supervision, with Positive Reinforcement and Constructive Feedback. Remember, whenever this change in behavior occurs, we respond with positive reinforcement. Even if the person has seemingly ignored the previous actions and warnings, we should be ready to accept the change whenever it happens. Otherwise, we're really in to punishment—"they should have come around earlier!"

65. *Don't let "Warm Bodies" turn dreams into nightmares.*

If we keep warm bodies just to fill a vacancy, we're creating a pattern that will haunt us for a long time. If termination is indicated, the vacancy is better than the warm body filling it—and influencing the whole workplace. "We keep Chuck around, even though he's not really doing the job. He's been here a long time and everybody knows what he can and can't do—which isn't much. But he's a nice enough guy." The first question is, "Why has he been around a long time if he's not doing the job?" The second question is, "Why do we have so much money in the budget that we can afford to keep someone who's not carrying his weight?" The third question is, "What message are we sending to the other employees who are doing the part of Chuck's job which he's not doing?"

66. *Discipline if necessary, but don't complain if you don't.*

At the water cooler, "You think you have a bad employee. You oughta hear about mine!" Don't talk to others about a poor performer; talk to the employee. It's a sign of poor supervision when we'd rather gripe about a bad employee than take the necessary action to correct the problem. Discipline certainly isn't the most pleasant thing we have to do. Telling someone they're doing a good job is more fun, makes both the employee and me feel good. Telling someone he or she is doing a poor (below standard) job is no fun, and it may make both of us feel bad. However, keeping a poor performer without taking necessary action makes the whole organization feel bad, including our bosses; and should make us unhappy, too. We have to deal with the problem!

67. *Take action quickly and decisively; don't ignore it.*

It seems easier to ignore the things that got us into formal discipline, but it's really the hard way out. Waiting will only aggravate the problem, not relieve it. It's even worse if we've started the formal discipline process, but stop after the "verbal or written warning." We're saying to the employee, "We really weren't serious about doing anything. Just keep on doing what you've been doing and we'll overlook it." We're also telling the other employees, "Fouling up isn't going to be much of a problem; we'll take this discipline process only so far, then stop it." It's always better to err on the side of action than on the side of inaction. If we have the facts, irrefutable, and the performance isn't meeting standards that have been explained and understood, we should calmly, with facts and documentation in hand, deal with the employee according to the organization's policy.

68. *Act, but don't overreact to poor performance.*

The longer we delay, the more frustrating it gets and the harder it is on us—and ultimately the poor performer. As we wait and do nothing, it's like an angry parent who keeps telling the two-year- old—with company sitting around—to stay away from the coffee table, but not taking any action. The kid keeps touching it, we keep warning, then in a burst of frustration, we grab the kid and the "fun begins." Up until then, the company wanted to grab us for not carrying out our threats. When we finally act, they feel sorry for the kid. Failing to take action on poor performance gets us in the same frame of mind. In our frustration we may overreact and overlook basic principles of discipline. We let our emotions get in the way of rational thinking. Our action may be too severe or our oral or written statements too biased.

69. *Realize that termination represents at least partial failure.*

If all other efforts fail to correct or change the behavior, our final step is termination. We have to admit that not all employees can be saved, or at least are not worth the effort and time it would take to get them to change their behavior. It's a failure in the sense that we've invested a lot of time, effort, and money in getting and keeping an employee on the payroll for however long they have been there. It also means that we will have to spend more money to hire and train another employee. Terminating someone causes us to feel bad because we know he or she is a real person with a real family, real bills, real car payments, etc. We may have some regrets for not spending more time or doing something differently to try to turn that person around or give him or her one more chance. Be that as it may, we need to learn from it and go on with our job.

70. *Realize that termination represents at least partial success.*

There is good that comes out of our decision to terminate an employee. For one thing, the organization is better off since the person who was not pulling the proper weight is gone. We're better off since we can now devote some time to the better employees, who deserve at least an equal amount of our time. The others aren't having to carry more than their share of the load, doing the work of the now-terminated employee (assuming we can replace the employee very soon). We may have learned some lessons about supervision, hiring, and about dealing with poor performers. That's a valuable lesson for later on. The fact is, many times employees who are terminated will admit it probably did them some good to understand that they have a responsibility to live up to standards, and that there is a consequence for not doing it.

71. *Don't let the law substitute for good supervision.*

Sometimes we may fail to take action against an employee for fear there will be legal ramifications. There may be ethnic, gender, or handicap considerations; but certainly the worst thing we can do is keep an unsatisfactory employee on board, knowing that he or she should be terminated, but not doing it for fear of the law. All of this can be prevented if we follow a few important steps. First, know the employee, do what's obviously fair, treat everybody the same, and know the law. In most cases, doing what's fair, will almost always meet the requirements of the law. The law protects not only the employee, but also the organization. Our dealings may have to include other departments, like Human Resources, since they are familiar with the rules and regulations. Still, we can't use the law as an excuse not to do what needs to be done when an employee is knowingly not doing his or her job.

101 Ways To Supervise Like A Human Being

Part Five:
Delegation

72. *Remember that Delegation is a skill that has to be learned.*

Knowing how to do a job is a different skill from knowing how to get others to do that job. It's more than common sense. It's more than just doing what comes natural. It's a skill unlike any we've been using doing the job itself, but it can be learned. Like any skill, it can be done well or poorly. Our task is to be certain we've learned it correctly. Admittedly, we don't have the skill of delegation when we first take over the job of getting others to do the job. It involves good communications; it involves good people skills; it involves knowing about motivation, since the ideal delegation is getting the employee not only to do the job, but also to be satisfied in doing it. It also requires that we understand some things about human nature. All these things can and should be learned.

73. *Moving up to a new job is like breaking up: It's hard to do.*

We often get promoted because we are doing the job so well, maybe even better than anyone else can do it. We know the job, the ins and outs, and all the intricacies of it, and we get a lot of satisfaction out of doing it. When we went home at night, we felt good about the job we had done and were proud of it. We got praise and recognition for it, even from higher management. The best thing of all was that out of it we got a promotion to supervision! But now, where has all the fun gone? It's even worse if we are now supervising the people we were working with, and in the group with the same production goals and procedures. Not the least of our problems is the fact that we no longer have us to depend on. We have lost the best worker, maybe replaced with a new or untrained person. To make it worse, we're new to our job, too! But the organization still has the same expectations of our group!

74. *We can do "it" better, but not "them" better.*

We see our people struggling with something we've assigned them—something we could easily do almost without thinking— we realize we could do it quicker and better and solve any problems that arise in doing it. Besides, it is something we used to get a lot satisfaction out of. The obvious thing to do is to step in—this time—and take over doing it. But, notice that we keep saying "it." Yes, we can do "it" better, faster, etc.; however, there are a lot of "its" out there and they become "them's". We can't do all the "them's" better, faster, smarter than anyone else. It's pretty obvious that if we were the best on the job, whoever takes over for us is not going to be doing the job as well as we did. That doesn't mean that they can't if they get good training and some experience. Each time we step in and do one of the "it's" we are prolonging the time when our people will be able to do it on their own.

75. *We need to get the job done through others.*

The simplest definition of "delegation" is, getting the job done through others. When we think about it, we realize that at one time we couldn't do the job either. Hopefully, somebody took us under his or her wing and had patience enough to let us learn and practice and even make mistakes. That "somebody" suffered just like we're suffering as we watch someone being slow and inaccurate and maybe even messing up. We have to turn it loose, still watching, but not doing. A major problem with our pitching in and doing it is that when we're doing someone else's job, no one is doing ours! Nobody is doing our scheduling, our budgeting, or our disciplining. It may well be that somebody above us is watching us and saying, "I could really do that supervisory job better, quicker. . . "

76. *Don't force responsibility on reluctant recipients.*

When we delegate, we are in effect giving people the power to be wrong. Total delegation is letting them have it and run with it because we still supervise, but we have several people doing several jobs, and we can't watch everything and everybody all the time. However, we have to be careful not to force people to take on things, especially responsibility, not spelled out in their job description. When we delegate something to someone that isn't part of their usual job, but fits within our power to delegate, we have to make certain that we aren't forcing them to take on an accountability they'd rather not have. They may be uneasy about adding this to their accountability. If there was no understanding that this is part of their job, we can't demand that they take responsibility for things that they don't want.

77. *Delegation as a good training tool.*

If we handle it correctly, delegation makes a great way to train people. In the early stages of the delegation there is less accountability, so the employees can feel safe in trying something they haven't done before. Gradually they take on more of the assignment and we do more and more training. No matter how complex or how simple the assignment is, we should always be thinking "training." "Dan, here's a small monthly report I've been doing for a long time. I think you would enjoy doing this. Would you like to watch me go through it next month and see how it's done?" We don't force the responsibility on Dan, and we show the training effort up front. If the assignment is a complicated one, of course there is more training.

78. *Delegate to lowest level of competency.*

With only a few exceptions, work should always be done at the lowest level of competency where it exists in my organization. Obviously, if the competency doesn't exist we can't delegate it. If it's a onetime assignment and we feel a certain employee has the potential to do it, we delegate and train, delegate and train until we've determined either that the person can do it or needs more development. We're always thinking, "Is there someone at a lower level who can do this?" When we do it this way, we're essentially putting more and more competency lower in the organization. It's like panning for gold; sometimes we find gold in unlikely places, sometimes in obvious places. Sometimes—when we don't even expect it—we find a very rich lode!

79. *Make delegation a challenge.*

There's a difference between a challenge and just plain dumping. If we only delegate to our best employees and if the assignments look alike most of the time, that's dumping. If we need something done accurately in a hurry and without supervision, and time after time we give it to our best person, it quits being a challenge. It's dumping. There's nothing wrong with giving our best employee a tough assignment, even a crash program with tight deadlines—that's a challenge. However, if we continue to do that over and over, and the assignments aren't very varied, it's still dumping. When we spread the work around, watch closely to see what hidden talents come out, and give the biggest challenges to the best people, that's delegation.

80. *Delegate only when we have the authority to do so.*

We can't delegate things like discipline or financial decisions which we have no authority to delegate, and there are things that need our input and are our accountability items. For example, we can't let others do our employee relations for us. Budgets and financial considerations may get inputs from lower levels, but the final accountabilities for submitting them lie with us. On the other hand, most of what we do can be delegated, with the limited authority to do it, if we are authorized to "get the job done, whatever it takes." Since authority also means accountability, we use caution in delegating it. But if it takes authority to get the final product out, then authority must accompany the delegation. There are other things we shouldn't delegate, and shouldn't have the authority to do! Discipline, for example, shouldn't be delegated to someone else. Praise for an excellent job should be done by us, and no one else.

81. *We keep what we delegate.*

Interestingly enough, nothing is actually given up when we delegate. If we are accountable for a special project or a routine activity, we will always be accountable for it. Even when we give the individual accountability for a task, and that person knows the blame or credit will come back to him or her, we still have the accountability for that assignment. If we define the responsibility areas for a work assignment, setting the limits and extent of the various parts, we still have the responsibility for each of these areas. As much as possible, when we delegate something to our people, we should do everything we can to let them have it as their own. Of course, we're there to answer questions, furnish needed information, but it should be thought of as theirs. However, we still have the right—and maybe need—to step in at anytime and handle whatever part needs us. Finally, we don't give up our authority when we pass it on to someone below us. We can still make and act on our own decisions if we need to.

82. *Give the necessary authority to do the job.*

Perhaps the hardest part of delegation is giving people the authority to make decisions and carry out certain tasks on their own. That's when we feel we've lost control. The moment we say, "It's all yours, but be sure to let me check everything before you turn it lose," we've kept the authority and are just giving out work. That's not really delegating. Authority is filled with helium: it tends to rise in the organization. It's much easier to give accountability than authority. People with authority seem more dangerous than people with accountability, because we use accountability as a leash. When we give them authority, we feel like the leash has been taken off. Hence, accountability is filled with lead—it tends to go down in the organization. We don't mind being able to blame people—that's accountability. We are afraid to give them power to act on their own—that's authority!

83. *Train employees before delegating accountability.*

People shouldn't be held accountable for things they don't know how to do, even if we've told them it's their job. Neither should they be held accountable for things they haven't been trained to do. It isn't a question of who does the training; it's a question of our seeing that the person gets trained, by whomever has the knowledge, skill and ability to train others in that knowledge and skill. We need to see the person doing it correctly, not just send them to a school or put them with someone who knows how to do the job. We should remember that when we delegate, they are going to be evaluated on how well they do it. If they didn't know how to do it in the beginning, and end up doing the job poorly, it's our fault, not theirs!

84. *Always tell employees what their responsibilities are.*

Responsibility is simply the actual tasks assigned to a person. The busboy cleans off the tables, the hostess seats the customers and operates the cash register, the waitress takes the orders, delivers the order to the kitchen and serves the cooked food. Each of these things is the assigned responsibility. They are the areas of work for each of the people. Both the amount of accountability and the amount of authority to make decisions is also determined for each area. If we aren't careful, we'll confuse "responsibility" with "accountability." Responsibility is what they do; accountability is how much blame or credit they get for doing it. Obviously, we also delegate certain decisions areas where they can do some things on their own.

85. *Match authority with accountability.*

This is the hard one. The best definition of real delegation is "the power or authority to act." If employees are expected to accomplish a task and will be held accountable for the results, they must have the authority to make the necessary decisions to do that task. It's pretty natural to throttle people with too much accountability and too little authority, but it's not right. We all like to have someone to blame and usually that's someone below me. "Hey, it's not my fault! I didn't tell them to do it that way!" The sad part is that it often works for us. We get off free, and the employee pays the price for the mistake. As difficult as it may be for us, we must be able to match the authority with the assignment we're going to hold the individuals accountable for. If we have the authority to give others the authority they need, and we expect the job to be done properly, it's only fair to give them all the tools to do the job correctly, including whatever authority it takes!

86. *Give our people the right to be wrong.*

We aren't making it acceptable for them to make mistakes, giving them the right to be wrong is still the best definition we have of delegation. If I check everything my people do, it's obvious that I'm going to correct things that are wrong or see that they correct them. The things that are okay go out as is. What that amounts to is that we've only given them the right to be right. What we actually did was give them work to do, but not the full responsibility for the final product. This isn't a case of throwing them in over their heads and letting them figure out how to swim; it's a matter of supervising their swimming lessons and making certain they know how to swim before allowing them to get into deep water. The analogy is that the people need training before we give them the right to be wrong. That means staying with them until they have demonstrated they can make the right decisions, solve particular problems related to the task, and feel comfortable with the authority to do the work.

87. *Give high achievers plenty of challenges.*

People who have been successful all their lives, expect to continue to be successful They don't need the encouragement or motivation of a lot of successes. They need difficult things to work on, and they'll stick with something till it's licked. They have the patience to spend long hours and deep thought on a project or task. They don't need nor expect a lot of praise for small accomplishments, but need and deserve adequate praise for difficult jobs done well. If we can avoid dumping on them with tedious tasks that are critical, but require little thought or problem solving, then we can delegate to these employees very successfully. In fact, we should be constantly looking for things to challenge them, especially things that will help them grow. Remember, these are the people we'd like to see running the organization in the years to come.

88. *Give low achievers plenty of successes.*

Those who have had very little success in life, school, or work, will need to have some meaningful successes. They don't have to be big successes nor extreme challenges. These people most likely will shy away from challenges that take a lot of time and thought just to finish a portion of the work. Because of their lack of previous successes, their tolerance for challenge is fairly low. We need to delegate things that will give them frequent, small successes. Hopefully, as they get more and more successes, we can increase the amount of challenge we delegate to them. We constantly monitor their feelings about what they are asked to do and make certain we don't scare them with too much, too fast. They will make good employees and often get excited over their small successes. After a while, they may start to ask for additional tasks with more challenge.

101 Ways To Supervise Like A Human Being

Part Six:
Managing Our Time

89. *We have enough time to do the job.*

We don't run out of time, we just let other lower priority items take up our time. If someone comes in the office or calls on the phone, we go ahead and handle the situation, even though it may be far down on our priority list—or not even on our list! Our argument may be, "The person was already there, or on the phone, and it only took a little bit of time, and it may save time later on. . ." But when we start to run out of time on a deadline, we will wish we had that "little bit of time" back. If we have fifteen phone calls a day and spend five minutes more than was necessary to conclude the business on each call, we lost an hour and fifteen minutes during the day. Even if these were high priority items, the time we lost wasn't productive on the priority item; it was just poor time usage.

90. *Do the top priorities first, or prove they weren't high priorities.*

We have a tendency to dread, even avoid high, tough priority items. We dread that unpleasant upcoming interview; we hate to make that call to the unhappy client; we would like to avoid telling the boss we blew it. So, what we do is work on a lower priority item that's easy, painless and maybe even fun. When we are finished, we have that feeling of accomplishment we like so well. The problem is that the high priority item didn't go away and may have gotten harder to handle because of our procrastination. We need some serious soul searching to decide if we still want it to be a high item. Maybe we can let it go and it'll disappear. That rarely happens, but it should be considered. Maybe we can break it into smaller, less painful bites. We could do part of the interview by telephone to get some advanced information; we could find something to offer the client temporarily; perhaps we could take the boss a solution at the same time we inform him or her that we messed up.

91. *Set our own priorities.*

Often we find people setting priorities for us; not just the boss but our co-workers, and maybe even our subordinates. "How about helping me out of this hole? I'm really hurting!" That's the voice of someone setting our priorities for us. It doesn't mean that we don't or won't help, but it does mean that we are going to check our own priorities and see if this effort will cause us to get behind in a high item. The most obvious things which let others set our priorities is the drop in or telephone caller. Someone sticks his or her head in the door and asks us a question on something that sounds innocent enough but soon becomes a major issue. We find ourselves going through our files, looking at stuff and giving advice. What looked innocent has grown into a major time consumer. The telephone is the same way. We answer the phone, find it's a friend who inquires about our health, then launch into a conversation that drags on in time and drags us into a problem that isn't dealing with anything that we need to be working on. The answer is to know our priorities and stop things before they get out of hand. "Hey, I'm sorry, but I'm pushing a deadline. Can I get back to you?"

92. *Be serious about how we make an item a top priority.*

Top priority list isn't just a priority list; it's a do-or-die list! We're telling ourselves, "Things at the bottom of this list may not get done, or they may not get done today. Things at the top of this list have to get done today, regardless!" But when we make up this list, setting priorities up and down the list, it's time for a reality check. The basic questions are: Is this really a top priority? Was it on the list yesterday and the day before, with nothing done on it? What will happen if it doesn't get done today? What will happen if it isn't done in several days? What will happen if it never gets done? One thing we find about our lists is that some of these things get on there because we just want to do them badly, or it's a pleasure doing them, or it will please someone else. Our questions will tell us whether or not the item belongs at the top. Part of the reality check is to ask ourselves if we really believe we will do this item first, or today, or ever. By the way, the final question to ask is whether or not we are the one who should be doing this at all. Are we taking up our own time doing someone else's job?

93. *Be honest in our planning.*

Make a legitimate plan. Not only do we determine if this is actually a high priority item, but let's also not fool ourselves into thinking we can do something in three hours when it will obviously take a whole day. Maybe, even if it is only a three-hour job, we put it on our daily work schedule for only an hour before the day is over. Will it take us extra time to start then stop, then start again tomorrow? Should we shift it back to an earlier starting time? We also have to ask ourselves if we have all the resources to carry out our plan of completion on the time schedule we would like. Is getting the information needed to finish the item a higher priority? Should that phone call tell us more than we know now? Should that phone call be a higher priority than the item we're looking at? Being honest with ourselves is often a very difficult feat!

94. *Nobody has more time than we do.*

We all get the same number of hours in each day, week, month, year, etc. It's not how many hours we have; it's how we assign the time to our work that counts. There is a saying that may or may not be true: "If you want to get something done, give it to a busy person." The idea is that a busy person is defined as someone who is supposedly making good use of time. The truth is, most of us procrastinate more than we realize. The estimate is that about eighty per cent of our work gets done in about twenty per cent of the time allotted for it. Most often that twenty per cent is the last part of the time set apart to do the work. We can use that extra time by crowding our schedule. We find that the end product isn't affected as much by the shorter time as we might think. As boring as it seems, people who get more done in the time allotted usually have made some kind of time study of their working habits. Where is my time going? What did I do that interfered with the work getting done more quickly? What got done in there that really didn't need to get done, or could have waited? This is a boring process; but if we do it honestly with ourselves, it pays off in great dividends.

95. *Make certain we're doing what needs to be done at the time.*

We pretty much always do what we want to do. Since we have a choice, we make the decision, based on the desired outcome. If we say we'd rather be playing golf than working on this project, that's not right, because we had a choice of which one to do. We chose work instead of golf because of the consequences. We decided we'd rather have the consequences of working on the project than those of playing golf. (Maybe keeping our job!) Hence, we're doing what we want to do. Now, since we have a choice, we need to make certain that the choice we make—which item on our priority list to work on—is really the most important thing to be doing right now! Even if it's reading this paragraph, is that the most important thing to be doing right now? Is a high priority item going by the wayside because we made the choice to read this instead of working on the project?

96. *Be busy doing what needs to be done.*

It's not enough just to be busy; we need to be busy doing the things that need to be done right now. "I can't get anything done because of all the interruptions," is an admission that we're busy doing someone else's job. "Busy" is a nebulous word. We can be busy doing unimportant things, or we can be busy doing things that just absolutely have to be done. From the outsider's point of view, we look just as busy either way. Only we can determine if our business is productive or wasted "busyness." Some of us are easily distracted by minute details. We hit a snag, get tired of the grind, find something that's interesting or needs to be done someday, or work on something that we're just curious about. Without realizing how fast time is going by, we get more interested in this side issue; and before we know it, a major part of our available time has slipped away. We were "busy" all that time. We may even been unaware that we'd eased into doing something that wasn't as important as the things we started out doing. Nevertheless, we've lost valuable time and have little to show for it. So we ask ourselves, "Am I doing the most important thing I should be doing right now?"

97. *Schedule unexpected interruptions.*

We need to have specified times for making and accepting phone calls, and to let people know these times. Drop people notes on some job we're doing that they may have questions about and simply say, "By the way, while I'm working on this I'm going to try to limit my telephone use to nine and ten o'clock in the morning and four to five in the afternoon. That'll give me a chance to finish this without interruptions. I'm sure I'll do a better job if I can concentrate on it." Of course, emergencies are always exceptions. If people call, let them know that you could be of more help to them if they'd give you time to finish what you're working on right now. Be polite, make it sound like a normal idea and one they would surely respect. Tell them when we're going to be available to talk to them. In other words, schedule our interruptions!

98. *Don't hesitate to tell people we're busy.*

When people call at a bad time or drop by the office, it's perfectly acceptable to let them know that we're busy at the moment. Isn't that rude? No, because if someone walks or calls into our space or time without invitation and without asking permission, that means several things: They don't think we're busy; they think their work is more important than ours; they don't mind being impolite; or they don't think about it at all. If they are thoughtless enough to interrupt us, it's all right for us to let them know—in a very nice way—that we are busy. We can also let them know that we will help them if it's a genuine emergency; but if it isn't, we can tell them when we'll have the time to help them. (Or as the joke goes: "So two o'clock won't work? How about tomorrow? No? Then how about never? Will that work for you—it would work fine for me!")

99. *Send interrupters a clear message.*

The message we want to send is three-fold: We're busy, we're organized, we want to help. How do we do that? Easily enough. "Hey, listen, I'm in the middle of something right now that's got a short deadline. Can I call you or come by around two o'clock? I'll be able to put some serious time in on your problem." What message does that send? First, it says, "I'm busy. I'm doing something that's important to me." It also says, "I'm organized. I know how long this is going to take and I know when I'll have time to work with you." Finally, it says, "I think your problem is important. I want to work on it when I'm able to give it my undivided attention, and I'll even call you or come by to see you about it." However, it also says, "It's your call; here's my choice of when I think I can do you the best job, but you decide how important your question is."

100. *Control time, not the other way around.*

If we live by the clock, we'll probably die by the clock. We set meetings by the clock. "The brainstorming meeting will be limited to an hour." That's pretty restrictive. We won't know the extent of brainstorming until we get into it. Maybe it would be better to say, "This will be an open ended meeting, but we'll try for an hour and see how we're doing." On the other hand, if the people attending the meeting are on the clock or have deadlines on their job, we may really need to limit the meeting to an hour. "Since we're all involved in other important things, we'll limit the session to an hour and schedule another meeting if we aren't finished. When someone calls or drops by and says, "Got a minute?" we look at the clock and say, "Yeah, I've got about ten minutes to spare. This stuff has to get out this afternoon." Or we may need to say, "Actually, I don't right now, but if you'll let me finish this, I can give you a lot more time."

101. *Quit early if we're finished.*

Sometimes we set a time frame, then finish earlier than we think we're going to. Unbelievably, we may keep on going to fill in the time. We use up not only our time, but the time of the very person or people we asked to help us. If we have designated a specific time for a meeting or project and see we can finish earlier, by all means do it! We don't have to use up all the allotted time just because we estimated it would take that long. (By the way, if it's going to take longer, and others are involved, we must be sure to get their permission to proceed beyond the announced time.) However, if we finish early, very few people will object strenuously if we let them out earlier than they expected. And that's true for this tip!

The End

Martin M. Broadwell
2882 Hollywood Drive
Decatur, GA 30033
404-292-3699

Carol Broadwell Dietrich
220 Old College Way
Atlanta, GA 30328
770-673-0515

About the Authors

Martin Broadwell began his twenty-year supervising career in the Bell System, leaving there as Director of Technical Training to devote full time to training supervisors and writing. Recognized by TRAINING Magazine as the "best supervisory trainer in the world" as they inducted him into the HRD Hall Of Fame in 1990, Martin was named the "Father of Training" by the University of Michigan's Executive Management Institute, after twenty-seven consecutive years of conducting seminars there." Martin has written fourteen books on leadership, supervision and training, including Moving Up To Supervision, The New Supervisor, Making Experience Pay, Supervising Today, and Supervising Technical and Professional People. This new book, 101 Ways to Supervisor Like a Human Being, co-written with his daughter and training companion for over twenty years, Carol Broadwell Dietrich, is a unique handbook and condensation of several of their books.

Carol Broadwell Dietrich has been a supervisor with two airlines and served with Delta Airlines as an instructor/advisor when they integrated Pan American Airlines into their organization. She is president of Training Systems International, Inc., a firm that provides leadership development assistance for numerous company and governmental entities, including such varied organizations as Frito Lay, Winn-Dixie Foods, Mead Paper Company, Colonial Pipeline, Continental Airlines, Centers for Disease Control and Prevention, U. S. Army Corps of Engineers (Germany and the U. S.), and several computer service companies. She has spent over twenty years in consulting in the areas of needs analysis, program development, implementation and evaluation, primarily in leadership development. Carol is the co-author of "The New Supervisor, How to Thrive in the First Year of Management." She also has written several articles for national magazines, and appeared on her own call-in talk show as a workplace consultant.